T0368462

the

KENNETH DAVID BRUBACHER

Book of Truth and Wisdom

the

KENNETH DAVID BRUBACHER

Book of Truth and Wisdom

A VERY SLENDER VOLUME

The Book of Truth and Wisdom

AuthorHouse™
1663 Liberty Drive
Bloomington, IN 47403
www.authorhouse.com
Phone: 1 (800) 839-8640

Art by darci-que™

Published by AuthorHouse 12/08/2015

ISBN: 978-1-5049-6400-5 (sc)
ISBN: 978-1-5049-6402-9 (hc)
ISBN: 978-1-5049-6401-2 (e)

Library of Congress Control Number: 2015919643

Print information available on the last page.

Any people depicted in stock imagery provided by Thinkstock are models, and such images are being used for illustrative purposes only.
Certain stock imagery © Thinkstock.

This book is printed on acid-free paper.

authorHOUSE®

ALSO BY KENNETH DAVID BRUBACHER

The Watcher

The Poor Shoemaker

Fly

Mennonite Cobbler

There's An Angel Under My Bed

Amos and Salina Go To Town

Leafy and Sprucy

Fire Dragon Moon

Commotion in the ManureYard

This Book is Dedicated to:

The Dyslexic Agnostic Insomniac

Who Lay Awake at Night

Wondering if there Really Is a Dog

the True Meaning of Life

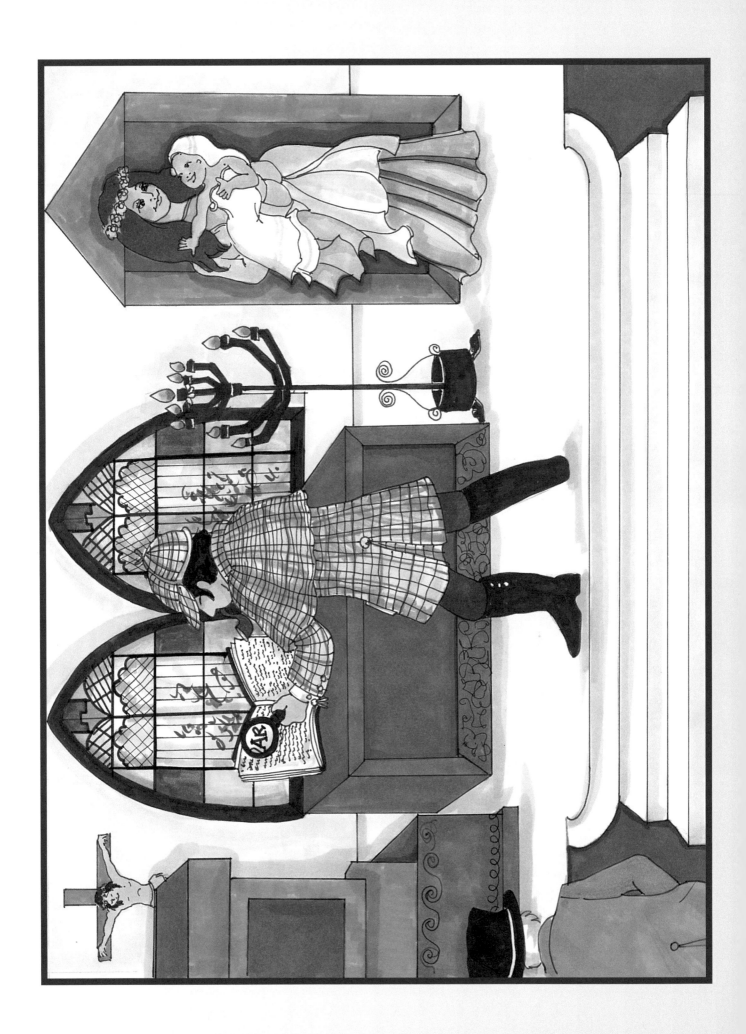

There once was a man

Who sought for

The True Meaning of Life

But he could not find it

He tried religions

Pretty much every one of them

But his spirit

Was still thirsty

Then he embraced

Many kinds of philosophy

But they   too

Left his soul hungry

He tried large amounts of

Pills   powders and potions

But they just

Gave him a headache

Then another man said

Ask The Old Man on the Mountain

He Knows

The True Meaning of Life

Our Seeker asked

Where shall I find him

The man pointed

Up there   On the mountain

So our Searcher

Who had declared Open Season

In the hunt for Truth

Mounted an expedition

He hired strong men

Who had skill in mountains

With animals to carry their stuff

And set out for the mountains

It did not go well

There were storms and blizzards

Cliffs and crapouts and crevasses

Avalanches and landslides

All his men and animals with all his stuff

Were swept away

With his next to dying gasp

he clambered onto a ledge

There was a very old man

In purple robe and flowing grey beard

Sitting in the lotus position

Meditating on the mountain

Are you

The Old Man on the Mountain

The old man said   I am

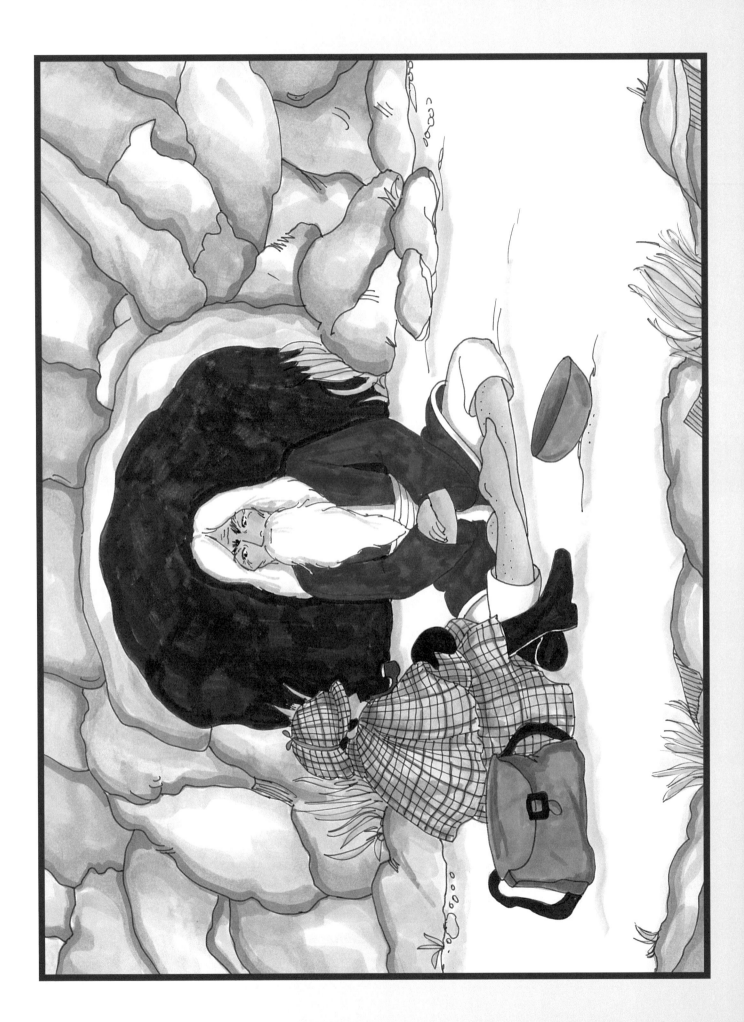

They say you know the True Meaning of Life

Yes he said I do

Then tell me Wise Sir

Before I die Please show me

The True Meaning of Life

My son I will tell you

The True Meaning of Life

Is the White Dove of Peace

Winging its beautiful path

Out over the endless seas of eternity

What said our Seeker hows that

No No that's not it at all

Oh my goodness

Replied The Old Man on the Mountain

Is this true?

Wisdom

If pen were put

To experience and knowledge

Mayhap mine be

A fairly hefty Tome

Of useful skills

Perhaps a score or so

Of pages   large of font
Lines well spaced

But wisdom

Alas

That be a slender volume

The World is Too Much With Us

By
William Wordsworth

The world is too much with
	us; late and soon,

Getting and spending, we
	lay waste our powers:

Little we see in Nature that is ours;
We have given our hearts
	away, a sordid boon!

This Sea that bares her bosom to the moon;

The winds that will be howling at all hours,

And are up-gathered now

like sleeping flowers;

For this, for everything, we are out of tune,

It moves us not. Great God! I'd rather be

A Pagan suckled in a creed outworn;

So might I, standing on this pleasant lea,

 Have glimpses that would

  make me less forlorn;

Have sight of Proteus rising from the sea;

Or hear old Triton blow his wreathèd horn.

ABOUT THE AUTHOR

Kenneth David Brubacher was born into a large family of sort of Mennonites in Elmira, ON, through no fault of his own. He was encouraged to make an attempt at becoming a normal human being, but with clearly limited success. To the surprise of nearly everyone he graduated from secondary school in 1970.

From there he traveled the world extensively, turning his hand to many kinds of jobs, and eventually returned to Elmira having accomplished very little. He got work as a millwright, but it was soon evident that he was a millwrong. After being mercifully fired from that job he went trucking and almost immediately distinguished himself (Summa Cum Laude with Oak Leaf Cluster and Silver Star) by destroying the truck.

He married and begat two lovely daughters who took after their mother in many wonderful ways, and turned out normal. It was considered a blessing that he had no sons because there was a high degree of probability that they might well grow up to be like their dad.

Knowing little about shoes, and even less about feet, he then took over his father's shoe repair shop and started to make shoes by hand along about April Fools' Day 1978. Very few people caught on. It was obvious that people whose feet were so bad that they sought out the services of a cobbler were not very fussy. The business prospered in spite of its inherent inadequacies.

He also applied himself to many varieties of sport, establishing a universal mediocrity in their pursuit seldom seen. When his body was sufficiently trashed he took up umpiring baseball, where it was observed that his training must have occurred under the tender administrations of the CNIB.

Currently he makes his home on a rented farm near Creemore, ON, and repairs a few shoes in his small shop in Collingwood. The farmhouse will soon become a gravel pit, whereupon it was his intent to establish institutions where Mennonites could go to seek quiet enjoyment. This, of course, until it was pointed out to him that they had already done it. These establishments are known as Mennonite Farms.

The author heartily recommends that any reader who takes a notion to write and produce a book or a play, then to lie down on the couch and watch videos of fawns gamboling in a sun-splashed meadow full of butterflies - until the feeling goes away.

It is hoped that you enjoy the book, and that its contents and presentation may provide therapeutic assistance in the remedy of your insomnia.

Printed in the United States
By Bookmasters